Pasta

BARNES
&NOBLE
BOOKS
NEW YORK

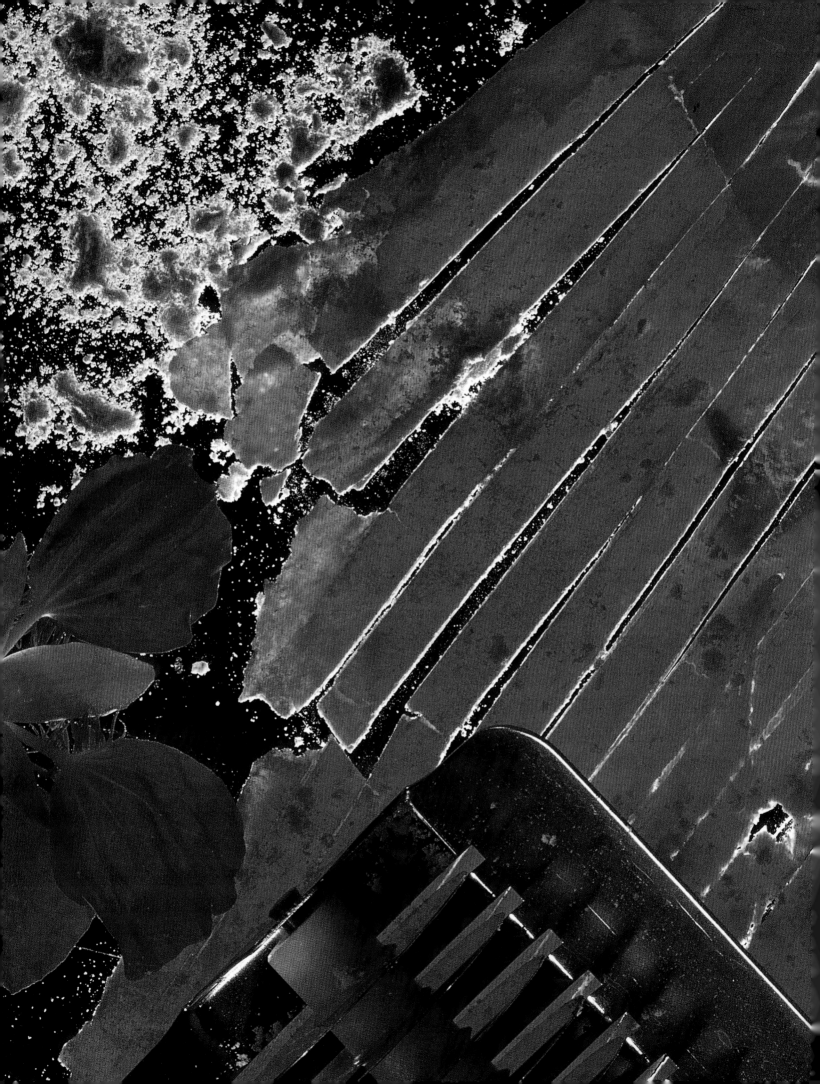

Contents

Spaghetti & Co.
An enticing variety

6

Step by Step
The essential cooking techniques

8

Pasta salads
From fusilli salad with radicchio to
tortiglioni salad with squid

10

Vegetarian Pasta
From farfalle (butterfly pasta) with sorrel sauce
to spaghetti with Sicilian vegetables

28

Pasta with Fish and Meat
From conchiglie (pasta shells) with trout and
fennel to spaghetti with a lemon and lamb ragout

56

Stuffed Baked Pasta
From cannelloni stuffed with vegetables to
spinach lasagne with tomato sauce

80

Spaghetti & Co.
An enticing variety

Noodles, or pasta, as it is called in Italy, come in every conceivable variety. It is also still a matter of dispute whether pasta was invented in China or in Italy. One thing there is no doubt about, however, is that the Italians are the real specialists where pasta is concerned; it is hard to think of a pretty shape – shells, little horns, little ears or snails – that has not been immortalized in a type of pasta. There are said to be more than 300 different kinds available. With such an abundance of choice, no wonder the question, "Which sort of pasta goes best with which sauce?" is now practically a science in its own right. One rule of thumb is: the heavier the sauce, the wider the pasta. That means, for example, that the ideal accompaniment to most meat sauces is a wide ribbon pasta such as pappardelle. Short types, such as penne or rigatoni, also go well with richer meat or vegetable sauces. The "long" types, spaghetti and macaroni, can be combined with almost any sauce, but are best suited to aromatic herb or tomato sauces.

PAPPARDELLE (left) comes from Tuscany, and is the widest of the various flat ribbon types.

1 SPAGHETTI literally means "pieces of string". It comes in various diameters and lengths (typically about 1 foot long). Thinner spaghetti is called spaghettini or vermicelli.

2 LASAGNE is made from semolina flour and can also be made with spinach, which gives it a green color. The no-boil variety has the advantage of not requiring pre-cooking.

3 FUSILLI look like little corkscrews, and because of their shape are ideally served with creamy sauces.

4 TAGLIATELLI is the classic pasta from the Parma region. The flat ribbons are narrower than pappardelle, and are often colored with spinach or tomato purée and served in the shape of a nest.

5 CONCHIGLIE are pasta shells. The small ones are very good for holding sauces, while the large ones are especially suitable for stuffing and oven-baking.

6 ROTELLE are often used in soups. They are shaped like cartwheels, and come in a variety of sizes.

7 MACARONI is a long, tubular pasta which comes from Naples. In Italy it is broken up before cooking, because its length makes them awkward to eat.

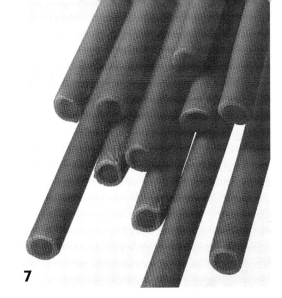

7

CANNELLONI also exist, like lasagne, in the no-boil variety. The large pasta tubes can be stuffed with a variety of fillings, then covered in sauce and oven-baked.

FARFALLE are called pasta butterflies because of their shape. Small farfalline are often used in soups.

FETTUCCINE, a flat ribbon pasta about ½-inch wide, is the Roman version of tagliatelle.

LINGUINE and **TRENETTE** look almost like spaghetti. They are not round, however, but pressed slightly flat.

PENNE are short pasta tubes which are cut off diagonally at the ends. They are available either smooth (penne lisce) or ridged (penne rigate).

RAVIOLI are stuffed pasta parcels, which can be bought fresh or dried, but of course taste best when they are home-made.

RIGATONI and **TORTIGLIONI** are names for short, thick pasta tubes with a ridged surface. They differ from penne in that they have a larger diameter and straight ends.

6

Step by Step
The essential cooking techniques

There is an enormous amount of ready-made pasta on the market, yet as all true pasta-lovers know, the homemade kind tastes better. True, it takes a certain amount of time and energy to prepare, but the hard work pays off in the end! The key to preparing pasta dough is the quality of the flour. Pasta pros use farina di semola fine (available in Italian delicatessens) or another coarse-grained flour such as Viennese Griessler. For those who prefer a grainy pasta, the flour should be mixed with semolina. Pasta dough must always be rolled out as thinly as possible. This used to be done with a rolling-pin; nowadays the job is usually left to a pasta machine. So that the pasta arrives at the table al dente, in other words firm to the teeth, it needs to be cooked not only for the right amount of time, but also in plenty of water. You should calculate about 1 quart of water to every ¼ pound of pasta. A dash of oil in the water will prevent home-made pasta from overcooking. Only if it is to be used in a salad should the pasta be rinsed in cold water, because this destroys the film of starch which helps the sauce cling to the surface of the pasta.

How to prepare pasta dough

1 Take 1 cup each of all-purpose flour and semolina, or just 2 cups all-purpose flour, and mix together on the work surface with ½ teaspoon of salt.

2 Make a wide well in the middle of the flour with your fingers. Break three eggs into the well, together with one tablespoon of oil.

3 Beat the eggs with the fork, at the same time incorporating some flour from the inside of the well. If the dough seems dry, add several tablespoons of water.

4 Knead with the balls of your thumbs from the outside inwards until a smooth, malleable dough is formed.

5 Ideally the dough should come easily off the worktop and have a slight shine on the surface.

6 Form the dough into a ball, cover it with a cloth and leave it to rest in a warm place for about 30 minutes.

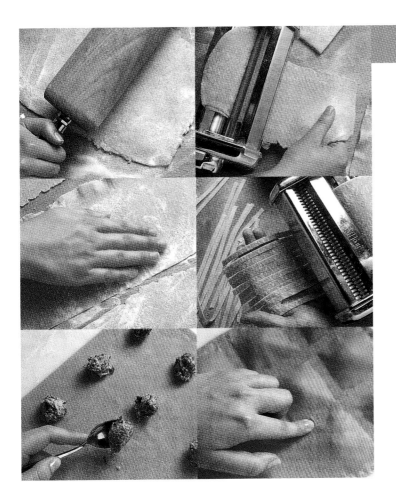

Making pasta shapes

1 On a floured work surface, roll the ball of dough out thinly with a rolling pin, starting in the middle and working outwards.

2 Thin the dough through the pasta machine, reducing the roller setting each time until the dough reaches the required thickness.

3 Sprinkle the thin pieces of dough with some flour and lay on a teatowel to dry for a short time.

4 Use a knife or the pasta machine on the appropriate setting to cut the pasta into ribbons of your chosen width.

5 For ravioli, place stuffing on half the piece of pasta, and fold the other half over it.

6 Press the dough in around the stuffing, then cut the ravioli out and pinch the edges together with a fork.

How to cook pasta

1 Bring about 1 quart of water to the boil for every ¼ pound of pasta in a large saucepan.

2 Add 1 slightly heaped teaspoon of salt per quart of water and put in the pasta.

3 While the pasta is cooking, stir it from time to time to prevent it from sticking together.

4 Cook for the time stated in the instructions on the package, and test the pasta to see if it is cooked.

5 As soon as the pasta is al dente, drain it in a colander.

6 Immediately mix with your chosen sauce, or toss in butter.

Pasta Salads

Spaghetti Salad
with a Herb and Cream Sauce

The ideal snack for warm summer evenings: Pasta lovers can't get enough
of this piquant salad with lots of fresh herbs

Ingredients

½ lb **spaghetti**

salt

2 **shallots**

1 bunch fresh **tarragon**

1 bunch fresh **dill**

1 bunch fresh **chives**

1 small organically grown **orange**

1 cup **sour cream**

2 tablespoons **lemon juice**

2 tablespoons **olive oil**

freshly ground **black pepper**

1 pinch **cayenne pepper**

2 cloves **garlic**

Preparation
SERVES 4

1 Following the instructions on the package, cook the spaghetti in plenty of boiling water until it is al dente. Strain into a sieve, rinse thoroughly with cold water and leave to drain.

2 Peel and finely dice the shallots. Wash the herbs and shake dry. Lay a few sprigs of tarragon aside for decoration, and pull the leaves off the remaining sprigs. Then remove the leaves from the dill, and chop finely with the tarragon. Cut the chives – up to about six sprigs – finely.

3 Scrub the orange in hot water and dry with paper towels. Remove half the peel with a zester. Cut the fruit in half, squeeze, and add the juice to a large bowl containing the sour cream, lemon juice, oil, salt, pepper and cayenne pepper, stirring the ingredients together to form a sauce. Peel and press the garlic cloves and add them to the mixture.

4 Stir the chopped dill, tarragon, and the chives and diced shallots into the sauce.

5 Add the spaghetti, mix with the sauce and leave to stand for about 15 minutes. Arrange the salad on a dish and garnish with the remaining herbs and the orange zest.

If you do not have a zester, you can use a kitchen knife to remove a thin layer of peel from the orange and cut them into fine strips.

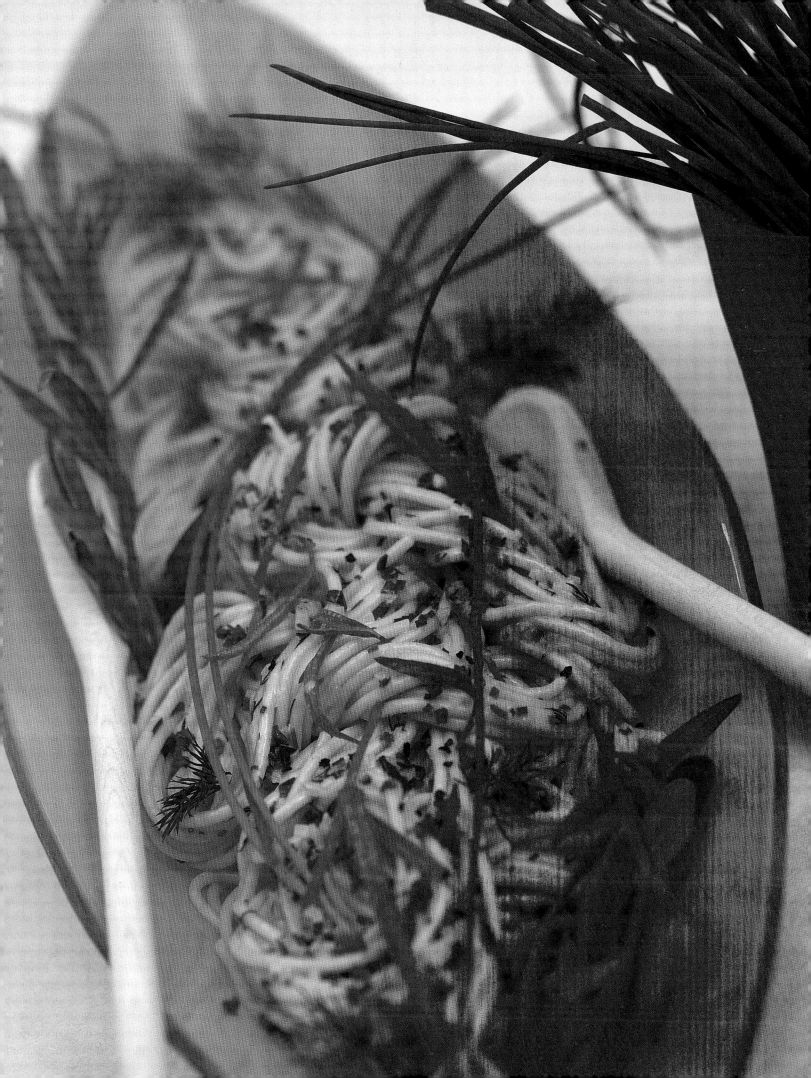

Fusilli Salad
with Radicchio

A salad that tastes of vacation: this refined pasta creation with radicchio,
salami and mozzarella will be a hit at any summer party

Ingredients

½ lb fusilli · salt

¼ lb salami (in slices)

6 pickled green chilies

4 stalks celery, with leaves

1 head radicchio

¼ lb mozzarella cheese

1 onion

4 tablespoons white wine
vinegar

⅓ cup olive oil

freshly ground black pepper

2 cloves garlic

½ cup black olives, pitted

Preparation
SERVES 4

1 Following the instructions on the package, cook the fusilli in plenty of boiling water until it is al dente. Strain into a sieve, rinse thoroughly with cold water and leave to drain.

2 Cut the salami into thin strips. Rinse the green chilies and cut into rings. Clean and wash the celery. Lay the leaves aside for decoration, then cut the celery into fine slices.

3 Clean the radicchio, separate it into individual leaves, then wash and dry in a spinner. Cut the mozzarella into small cubes. Peel and finely chop the onions.

4 Make a dressing by whisking the oil, vinegar, salt and pepper together in a large bowl. Peel and press the garlic cloves and add to the mixture.

5 Add the salami strips, chilies, sliced celery, onions, olives and half the mozzarella cubes with the pasta to the dressing in the bowl, and mix well.

6 Toss the pasta salad with the radicchio and celery leaves, scatter over the remaining cubes of mozzarella, and serve.

Garganelli Salad
with Broccoli and Tuna

Preparation
SERVES 4

1 Following the instructions on the package, cook the garganelli in plenty of boiling water until it is al dente.

2 Divide the tuna into rough chunks. Blanch the broccoli florets for about seven minutes in boiling, salted water, rinse with ice-cold water and leave to drain.

3 Wash and core the tomatoes, then cut into eighths. Peel and finely chop the shallot and the garlic.

4 Heat the oil in a frying pan, add the garlic and shallot and cook until transparent. Throw in the broccoli florets and tomato segments and cook for 5 minutes longer.

5 Drain the garganelli and mix with the broccoli and tomatoes. Season with salt, pepper and the vinegar. Carefully stir in the pieces of tuna, and leave to stand for at least 30 minutes. Serve with the Parmesan and basil.

Ingredients

½ lb **garganelli** or **penne rigate**

salt · 6-oz can **tuna**, in water

½ lb **broccoli** florets

½ lb **tomatoes** · 1 **shallot**

1 clove **garlic** · 3 tablespoons **olive oil**

freshly ground **black pepper**

1 tablespoon **white wine vinegar**

¼ cup freshly-grated **Parmesan cheese**

a few **basil leaves**, cut into fine strips

Ingredients

¾ lb **spaghetti**

salt

2 **red peppers**

4 **potatoes**

1 cup **olive oil**

1 lb baby **spinach**

⅔ cup **black olives**, pitted

2 tablespoons **balsamic vinegar**

1 teaspoon medium-hot **mustard**

2 cloves **garlic**

freshly ground **black pepper**

Spaghetti Salad
with Spinach and Potatoes

Preparation
SERVES 4

1 Cook the spaghetti until it is al dente. Strain into a sieve, rinse with cold water and leave to drain.

2 Halve the red peppers lengthways, core and seed them, then wash and cut into rough pieces. Peel the potatoes, wash and dice finely.

3 Heat three tablespoons of oil and brown the potato. Add the peppers and brown them with the potato.

4 Clean and wash the spinach, then blanch in boiling salted water. Strain, rinse with ice-cold water, and leave to drain thoroughly. Halve the olives. Mix all the salad ingredients together in a large bowl.

5 For the dressing, stir the balsamic vinegar together with the mustard and salt. Peel and press the garlic and add to the mixture. Whisk in the remaining oil, season the dressing with pepper and drizzle over the salad.

Penne Salad
with Salsa Verde

Salsa verde, the original green sauce from Italy,

may not be as well-known as pesto, but it's just as aromatic

Ingredients

½ lb **penne rigate** · **salt**

1 bunch fresh **chives**

1 bunch fresh **basil**

1 bunch fresh flat-leaf **parsley**

a few sprigs each of **oregano**
and **thyme**

3 tablespoons **balsamic vinegar**

4 tablespoons **olive oil**

1 teaspoon medium-hot **mustard**

freshly ground **black pepper**

2 cloves **garlic**

Preparation
SERVES 4

1 Following the instructions on the package, cook the penne in plenty of boiling water until it is al dente. Strain into a sieve, rinse with cold water and leave to drain.

2 Wash the chives then shake them dry and cut into small sections. Wash the basil, parsley, oregano and thyme and shake them dry. Pull off the leaves, retaining a few for decoration, and chop the remainder finely.

3 Make a dressing by stirring the balsamic vinegar together with the oil, mustard, salt and pepper in a large salad bowl. Peel and press the garlic, and add to the mixture.

4 Stir the chopped herbs into the dressing. Add some more salt and pepper.

5 Put the penne into the bowl, mix with the herb dressing and leave to stand for about 15 minutes. Garnish with the remaining herbs and serve.

The aroma of fresh herbs can be best released by chopping them finely with a chopping knife. Cutting them with an ordinary knife tends to crush the leaves.

Spaghetti Salad
with Tuna Sauce

A dish to make a gourmet's heart sing – this refined, colorful summer salad
is quick to prepare and so right for a satisfying meal

Ingredients

½ lb **spaghetti** · salt

1 lb **green beans**

1 bunch **scallions**

6-oz can **tuna**, in water

10 **cherry tomatoes**

2 tablespoons **white wine vinegar**

⅓ cup **olive oil**

1 teaspoon hot **mustard**

2 tablespoons **crème fraîche**
or sour cream

freshly ground **black pepper**

sugar

1 tablespoon dried **thyme**

1 **lemon**

Preparation
SERVES 4

1 Following the instructions on the package, cook the spaghetti in plenty of boiling water until it is al dente. Strain into a sieve, rinse with cold water and leave to drain.

2 Snip off the ends from the beans and pull off any strings from the seams. Wash the beans, break into 2 to 3-inch pieces and cook for about 10 minutes in plenty of boiling water.

3 Clean and wash the scallions, then cut them into fine rings. Drain the tuna fish and pull apart into small pieces. Wash and quarter the cherry tomatoes.

4 Stir together the oil, vinegar, mustard and crème fraîche to form a dressing, then season with salt, pepper and sugar.

5 Strain the beans into a sieve, allow to drain and immediately mix with the dressing. Stir in the thyme and pieces of tomato and tuna.

6 Place the spaghetti onto a large dish and arrange the tuna and bean mixture on top. Cut the lemon into eighths, garnish the salad with the lemon segments, and serve.

Tortiglioni Salad
with Squid

This dish tastes of the sea: with squid, anchovies and garlic it brings back memories of vacations in the sunny south

Ingredients

½ lb **tortiglioni** or other short tube pasta

salt

2 **red peppers**

1 clove **garlic**

4 **anchovies** in oil

½ cup **olive oil**

juice of one small **lemon**

1 tablespoon dried **oregano**

freshly ground **black pepper**

1 lb **squid**, cleaned

1 bunch fresh **basil**

Preparation
SERVES 4

1 Following the instructions on the package, cook the tortiglioni in plenty of boiling water until it is al dente. Strain into a sieve, rinse with cold water and leave to drain.

2 Turn on the broiler. Halve the peppers lengthwise, clean, wash and lay skin side upwards onto a baking sheet. Cook the peppers for about 10 minutes on the middle shelf of the oven, until the skin is brown and blistered. Transfer the peppers to a plastic bag and leave to cool for 10 minutes, then skin them and cut into narrow strips of equal size.

3 Peel the garlic and purée in a blender or food processor, together with the anchovies, 3 tablespoons of the oil, the lemon juice and oregano. Put the sauce into a large bowl. Season lightly with salt and pepper.

4 Wash the squid, dry with paper towels, and cut into rings. Heat the remaining oil in a frying pan. Add the squid and cook for just 2 minutes. Season with salt and pepper. Add to the bowl with the garlic sauce along with the red pepper and tortiglioni and mix thoroughly.

5 Wash the basil and shake it dry. Pull the leaves off the stems, reserve a few for decoration and chop the remainder finely. Mix the chopped basil leaves into the salad. Arrange the salad on a dish and serve garnished with the reserved basil.

22

Rotelle Salad
with Salami and Arugula

Preparation
SERVES 4

1 Following the instructions on the package, cook the rotelle in plenty of boiling water until it is al dente. Strain into a sieve, reserving about one cup of the cooking water. Rinse the rotelle in cold water and leave to drain.

2 Remove the thin brown rind from the scamorza and cut the cheese into small cubes. Also cut the salami into small cubes and mix both with the pasta.

3 Stir the mayonnaise together with the mustard, salt and pepper, then add the lemon juice, horseradish, oil and vinegar. Stir the cheese and salami into the mayonnaise mixture. Stir in the reserved pasta cooking water and leave the salad to stand for at least 30 minutes.

4 Shortly before serving, clean the arugula. Roughly chop the leaves and stir them into the salad.

Ingredients

½ lb **rotelle rigate** · **salt**

¼ lb **scamorza** or **mozzarella cheese**

3 oz Genoa **salami**

4 tablespoons **mayonnaise**

1 teaspoon **mustard** flavored with herbs

freshly ground **black pepper**

juice of 1 **lemon**

1 tablespoon grated **horseradish**

1 tablespoon **balsamic vinegar**

1 tablespoon **walnut oil**

1 bunch **arugula**

Ingredients

¾ lb **farfalle**

salt

4 **beef tomatoes**

½ lb **mozzarella cheese**

10 **black olives**, pitted

1 bunch fresh **basil**

⅓ cup **olive oil**

2 cloves **garlic**

freshly ground **black pepper**

Farfalle Salad
with Tomatoes and Olives

Preparation
SERVES 4

1 Following the instructions on the package, cook the farfalle in plenty of boiling water until it is al dente. Strain into a sieve, rinse with cold water and leave to drain.

2 Pour boiling water over the tomatoes, let sit for 5 minutes, then skin them. Dice the tomatoes into small pieces. Cut the mozzarella into small cubes. Quarter the olives. Wash the basil and shake dry, pull off the leaves and cut into fine strips.

3 Heat the oil in a deep frying pan, add the peeled garlic cloves and fry until golden brown. Remove the garlic from the frying pan.

4 Toss the farfalle briefly in the garlic oil, and place in a large bowl. Add the diced tomato and mozzarella, olive pieces and basil, and mix thoroughly. Season the salad generously with salt and pepper.

Spaghetti Salad
with Avocado and Shrimp

A touch of luxury: The fine seafood in this extravagant salad ensures
that it appeals to even the most demanding palate

Ingredients

½ lb **spaghetti**

salt

2 **avocados**

juice of 1 **lemon**

1 clove **garlic**

2 tablespoons **olive oil**

freshly ground **black pepper**

1 **red chili**

½ lb **shrimp**

3 teaspoons **green peppercorns**
in brine

Preparation
SERVES 4

1 Following the instructions on the package, cook the spaghetti in plenty of boiling water until it is al dente. Strain into a sieve, rinse in cold water and leave to drain.

2 Halve the avocados lengthways and remove the stones. Peel the avocado halves and halve again. Squeeze lemon juice over one quarter and reserve it in the refrigerator.

3 Peel the garlic clove and, together with the remainder of the avocados, the oil and the rest of the lemon juice, purée in a blender or food processor. Pour the avocado sauce into a large bowl, and add salt and pepper.

4 Mix the spaghetti with the sauce and let stand for a short time. Meanwhile halve the chili lengthwise, core and wash it, then cut it into narrow strips.

5 Wash the shrimp in cold water and dry with paper towels. Mix in with the pasta, along with the strips of chili and peppercorns.

6 Cut the reserved avocado quarter into slices. Arrange the salad on a platter and garnish with the avocado slices.

Green peppercorns are pepper fruits harvested when they are still green and unripe. They have a milder flavor than black pepper, and are sold either in brine or freeze-dried.

Vegetarian Pasta

Spaghetti
with Mushrooms and Mint

Not an everyday combination: All kinds of mushrooms and fresh mint,

a delight for the tastebuds that is not to be missed

Ingredients

1 ½ lbs mixed fresh **mushrooms**
(depending on the season,
ordinary mushrooms, shiitake
mushrooms, oyster mushrooms,
chanterelles or porcini)

3 sprigs of **mint**

salt

1 lb **spaghetti**

2 **shallots**

4 tablespoons **olive oil**

1 clove **garlic**

freshly ground **black pepper**

Preparation
SERVES 4

1 Wipe the mushrooms with paper towels, and if necessary, wash. Leave smaller mushrooms whole, or cut in half. With larger mushrooms, twist the stems out of the caps and cut into small pieces. Cut the caps crosswise in slices.

2 Wash the mint, shake it dry, and then remove the leaves from the stems. Set aside a few leaves for decoration and finely chop the remainder.

3 Bring plenty of water to the boil, add salt and cook the spaghetti according to the instructions on the package until it is al dente.

4 Meanwhile peel the shallots and chop finely. Heat the oil in a frying pan, add the shallots and cook until transparent. Add the mushrooms and cook with the shallots briefly, about 5 minutes.

5 Peel and press the garlic and add to the mixture. Throw in the chopped mint and allow all the ingredients to cook together over a low heat for a few minutes. Season with salt and pepper.

6 Strain the spaghetti into a sieve and leave to drain. Mix with the mushroom ragout and serve garnished with the mint leaves.

30

Pappardelle
with Gorgonzola Sauce

Feel like trying an unusual creation? Pears and Gorgonzola:

A classic combination rediscovered for pasta

Ingredients

1 bunch **celery** with leaves

2 tablespoons **butter**

salt

1 lb **pappardelle**

½ lb **Gorgonzola cheese**

1 cup **heavy cream**

freshly ground **black pepper**

4 tablespoons **pine nuts**

1 small **pear**, such as Bartlett

Preparation
SERVES 4

1 Clean and wash the celery. Cut the stalks diagonally into thin slices, reserving the leaves for decoration.

2 Heat the butter in a saucepan, add the slices of celery and cook over a medium heat for about 5 minutes.

3 Bring plenty of water to the boil, add salt and cook the pappardelle according to the instructions on the package until it is al dente.

4 Meanwhile cut the Gorgonzola into small pieces. Set a few pieces aside, then add the remainder to the celery slices, along with the cream. Bring to the boil for a short time, and melt in the cheese over a low heat, stirring continuously. Allow the sauce to simmer briefly, season generously with salt and pepper.

5 Dry-roast the pine nuts in a frying pan until golden brown. Wash, halve, and core the pear, then cut into segments.

6 Strain the pappardelle into a sieve and allow to drain. Place in a bowl with the Gorgonzola sauce and pear segments, then scatter the roasted pine nuts and remaining pieces of cheese onto it. Garnish with the celery leaves, and sprinkle to taste with coarsely ground pepper.

The sauce will be even more piquant if instead of Gorgonzola you use Roquefort, which has a stronger flavor. For a milder sauce, use a mixture of Gorgonzola cheese, cream cheese, and mascarpone.

Macaroni
with Spinach and Ricotta Sauce

Preparation
SERVES 4

1 Clean and wash the spinach. Blanch for a short time in boiling salted water, squeeze out well and chop roughly.

2 Bring plenty of water to the boil, add salt, drop in the macaroni and cook according to the instructions on the package until it is al dente.

3 Meanwhile heat the oil in a saucepan, add the chopped spinach and braise briefly. Peel and press the garlic, add it to the spinach and season with salt, pepper and nutmeg.

4 Stir the raisins into the spinach and cook the two together for a short time. Dry-roast the pine nuts in a frying pan until golden brown.

5 Strain the macaroni into a sieve and allow to drain. Place in a preheated dish with the butter and the spinach.

6 Scatter the pine nuts and roughly chopped ricotta on top, and once more mix all the ingredients well.

Ingredients

1 lb baby **spinach**

salt

2 tablespoons **olive oil**

2 cloves **garlic**

freshly ground **black pepper**

1 pinch freshly grated **nutmeg**

1 lb **macaroni**

⅓ cup **raisins**

3 tablespoons **pine nuts**

1 tablespoon **butter**

⅔ cup **ricotta cheese**

Ingredients

5 slices **smoked bacon**

½ cup **black olives**

1 **shallot**

salt · 1 lb **pappardelle**

2 tablespoons **olive oil**

1 clove **garlic**

3 sprigs fresh **basil**

1 teaspoon **cornstarch**

6 tablespoons **vegetable stock**

1 cup freshly grated **Parmesan cheese**

freshly ground **black pepper**

Pappardelle
with Olive and Basil Sauce

Preparation
SERVES 4

1 Cut the bacon into fine strips. Halve and stone the olives and cut into fine strips. Peel and finely chop the shallot.

2 Bring plenty of water to the boil, add salt, drop in the pappardelle and cook according to the instructions on the package until it is al dente.

3 Meanwhile heat the oil and cook the shallots in it until transparent. Add the bacon and brown in the oil.

4 Peel and press the garlic, and add to the pan. Stir in the olives and the washed and chopped basil leaves.

5 Add the cornstarch to the vegetable broth in a cup and stir together. Pour into the sauce and bring to the boil once. Stir in the Parmesan and season the sauce with salt and pepper. Strain the pappardelle into a sieve and mix with the sauce.

Fettuccine
with Peppers

The sort of pasta popular far beyond Sicily:

Peppers and fresh herbs bring vacation sunshine to every table

Ingredients

2 **yellow peppers**

2 **red peppers**

2 cloves **garlic**

1 bunch fresh **flat-leaf parsley**

1 bunch fresh **basil**

salt

1 lb **fettuccine**
(or tagliatelle)

1 tablespoon **butter**

½ cup **vegetable stock**

½ cup dry **white wine**

2 tablespoons **balsamic vinegar**

freshly ground **black pepper**

Preparation
SERVES 4

1 Halve the peppers lengthwise, seed and core. Wash the pepper halves and cut into fine strips. Peel the garlic cloves and chop finely.

2 Wash the parsley and basil, shake dry, then pull the leaves off the stems. Set aside a few basil leaves for decoration and finely chop the remainder.

3 Bring plenty of water to the boil, add salt, drop in the fettuccine and cook according to the instructions on the package until it is al dente.

4 Meanwhile heat the butter in a large frying pan, add the garlic and strips of pepper and cook for a short time. Pour in the vegetable stock and the white wine, and allow all the ingredients to cook for about 8 minutes. Sprinkle the peppers with balsamic vinegar and season with salt and pepper.

5 Strain the fettuccine into a sieve and allow to drain. Mix with the peppers in the frying pan and heat up for a short time. Stir the chopped herbs into the pan of pasta. Garnish with the reserved basil leaves and serve.

Aromatic, long-matured balsamic vinegar is not only an excellent ingredient for salad dressings. It also lends a distinctive flavoring to vegetable sauces.

Farfalle
with Sorrel Sauce

A pasta fantasy in green and white: Sorrel and butterfly pasta
combine to make an extravagant spring dish

Ingredients

1 large **cucumber**

1 small bunch **sorrel**

salt

1 lb **farfalle**

2 tablespoons **butter**

¼ cup shelled **pistachios**

⅔ cup full-fat **yogurt**

2 tablespoons **lime juice**

freshly ground **black pepper**

1 small organically grown **lime**

Preparation
SERVES

1 Wash the cucumber, cut in half lengthways and remove the seeds. Cut the flesh into fine strips. Wash the sorrel and shake dry. Set aside a few leaves for decoration, then cut the remainder into very fine strips.

2 Bring plenty of water to the boil, add salt, drop in the farfalle and cook according to the instructions on the package until the pasta is al dente.

3 Meanwhile melt the butter in a large frying pan, add the cucumber and cook for 5 minutes. Grind the pistachios in a food processor. Mix with the yogurt and lime juice and stir into the cucumber strips. Season generously with salt and pepper.

4 Strain the farfalle into a sieve, allow to drain and mix with the yogurt sauce. Arrange on plates with the reserved sorrel leaves, and scatter the strips of sorrel on top. Wash the lime in hot water, dry, and cut into segments. Serve the farfalle garnished with the lime segments and, if desired, with a few strips of lime zest.

The small strips of sorrel will release their fine, refreshing aroma even better if they are shallow-fried in hot oil for a short time before serving.

38

Penne
with Tomatoes and Pesto

Preparation
SERVES 4

1 To make the pesto, wash the basil, shake it dry and pull the leaves off the stems. Peel and halve three garlic cloves. Reserve a few basil leaves for decoration, then chop up the remainder in a blender, along with the garlic and pine nuts. Add ½ cup of the Parmesan and a pinch of salt, gradually pour in 6 tablespoons of the olive oil, and mix well.

2 Bring plenty of water to the boil, add salt, drop in the penne and cook according to the instructions on the package until the pasta is al dente.

3 Meanwhile wash and quarter the tomatoes, then cut into small dice. Heat the remaining oil in a large saucepan, add the tomatoes and cook. Peel and press the last garlic clove and add to the mixture. Stir in 6 tablespoons of the pesto and season with salt and pepper.

4 Strain the penne into a sieve, allow to drain, add to the tomatoes and heat for a short time. Garnish with the remaining Parmesan and basil leaves and serve. Keep the rest of the pesto in a screw-top jar in the refrigerator.

Ingredients

3 bunches fresh **basil**

4 cloves **garlic**

1 cup **pine nuts**

⅜ cup freshly grated **Parmesan cheese**

salt

½ cup **olive oil**

1 lb **penne lisce**

6 **tomatoes**

freshly ground **black pepper**

Ingredients

1 bunch **scallions**

1 organically grown **lemon**

salt

1 lb **spaghetti**

1 tablespoon **butter**

⅔ cup **pecorino cheese**

1 cup **heavy cream**

freshly ground **black pepper**

Spaghetti
with Pecorino Cheese

Preparation
SERVES 4

1 Clean and wash the scallions. Cut half the scallions into rings, and the remainder lengthways into narrow strips.

2 Wash the lemon in hot water and cut in half. Squeeze one half and cut the other into thin slices.

3 Bring plenty of water to the boil, add salt, drop in the spaghetti and cook according to the instructions on the package until the pasta is al dente.

4 Meanwhile melt the butter in a frying pan, add the scallion strips and cook until softened. In a food processor or blender, purée 3 tablespoons of the pecorino cheese with the cream and 1 tablespoon of lemon juice. Add to the frying pan, stir and simmer for a short time.

5 Season the sauce with salt and pepper and mix with the drained pasta. Garnish with scallion rings, lemon slices and the remaining pecorino cheese.

Spaghettini
with Sun-dried Tomatoes

A pasta dish that becomes addictive: Sun-dried tomatoes and

purslane give it a unique aroma

Ingredients

1 lb **scallions**

3 cloves **garlic**

1 cup **sun-dried tomatoes** in oil

salt

1 lb thin **spaghetti**

4 tablespoons **olive oil**

freshly ground **black pepper**

small bunch **purslane**

1 small chunk **pecorino cheese**,
about ¼ cup

Preparation
SERVES 4

1 Clean and wash the scallions and chop finely.

2 Peel and finely chop the garlic cloves. Allow the sun-dried tomatoes to drain on paper towels, then cut into fine strips.

3 Bring plenty of water to the boil, add salt, drop in the spaghettini and cook according to the instructions on the package until the pasta is al dente.

4 Meanwhile heat the oil in a large saucepan. Add the garlic, sun-dried tomatoes and scallions and cook for 8 minutes. Season with salt and pepper.

5 Wash the purslane, shake it dry and remove the leaves. Strain the spaghettini into a sieve and allow to drain. Mix with the tomatoes in the saucepan and heat up for a short time. Garnish with the purslane and slices of the pecorino on top.

Purslane should be as fresh as possible and should not be heated. As the herb is slightly salty, the pasta sauce should be seasoned carefully.

Penne
with a Herb and Cheese Sauce

Preparation

SERVES 4

1 Wash the parsley, shake dry and remove the leaves from the stems. Reserve a few for decoration, then roughly chop the remainder. Peel and halve the garlic cloves. Purée to a fine paste in a blender with the parsley, lemon juice, 3 tablespoons of the oil and the pine nuts.

2 Bring plenty of water to the boil, add salt, drop in the penne and cook according to the instructions on the package until the pasta is al dente.

3 Meanwhile roughly grate the Gouda and stir into the herb sauce along with the crème fraîche. Season generously with salt and pepper. Heat the remaining parsley leaves for 1 minute in 4 tablespoons of very hot oil.

4 Strain the penne into a sieve, allow to drain and mix immediately with the cheese and herb sauce. Serve garnished with the chives and fried parsley leaves.

44

Ingredients

2 bunches fresh **flat-leaf parsley**

1 clove **garlic**

1 tablespoon **lemon juice**

7 tablespoons **olive oil**

3 tablespoons **pine nuts**

salt

1 lb **penne lisce**

¼ lb medium-matured **Gouda cheese**, in one piece

2 tablespoons **crème fraîche** or sour cream

freshly ground **black pepper**

a few fresh **chives**

Ingredients

1 cup **brown lentils**

2 **tomatoes** · 1 **carrot**

1 stalk **celery**

2 cloves **garlic**

4 tablespoons **olive oil**

1 finely diced **onion**

1 **green chili**, chopped

½ cup dry **white wine**

salt · freshly ground **black pepper**

2 tablespoons **balsamic vinegar**

1 lb **linguine** (or spaghetti)

1 bunch **arugula**

Linguine
with Balsamic Lentils

Preparation
SERVES 4

1 Wash the lentils, cover with water and leave to soak overnight. Do not drain.

2 Wash the tomatoes, blanch them in boiling water, then peel them. Peel and finely dice the carrot. Wash the celery stalk and cut into fine slices.

3 Peel and finely chop the garlic cloves. Heat the oil in a large saucepan, add the diced onion, strips of chili and garlic, and allow to cook. Pour in the lentils along with the water they were soaked in, and the wine, and allow the mixture to simmer for 30 minutes. 10 minutes before the end of the cooking time, add the tomatoes, carrots, celery, and balsamic vinegar. Season with salt and pepper.

4 Following the instructions on the package, cook the linguine in plenty of boiling water until it is al dente. Clean and wash the arugula and dry in a spinner. Strain the pasta and allow to drain, then mix with the balsamic lentils and arugula.

Spaghetti
with Basil

Simple but unsurpassed: Aromatic garlic and herb oil and
strong cheese guarantee a unique taste experience

Ingredients

1 lb **spaghetti**

salt

4 bunches fresh **basil**

2 cloves **garlic**

½ cup **olive oil**

freshly ground **black pepper**

¼ cup **pecorino cheese**,
in one piece

Preparation
SERVES 4

1 Following the instructions on the package, cook the spaghetti in plenty of boiling water until it is al dente.

2 Wash the basil, shake dry and remove the leaves from the stems. Reserve about 20 leaves for decoration, then cut the remainder into fine strips. Peel the garlic cloves.

3 Meanwhile heat half the oil in a frying pan and cook the strips of basil until crisp, then crush and add the garlic to the frying pan.

4 Strain the spaghetti into a sieve and allow to drain. Add to the garlic and herb oil in the pan and mix well. Season with salt and pepper.

5 Heat the remaining oil in a second frying pan until it is very hot, then fry the reserved basil leaves in it for 1 minute. Allow to drain on paper towels, then add to the spaghetti mixture.

6 Arrange the pasta with the fried basil leaves on a dish, and use a cheese slicer to thinly slice the pecorino over the top.

Fried herb leaves have a very special aroma, and add the final touch to any dish. Another idea to try is sage leaves that have been dipped in batter and then fried.

Pappardelle
with Tomato and Arugula Sauce

A variation on a classic theme: As for many pasta sauces,

the best base is still homemade tomato sauce

Ingredients

3 bunches **arugula**

2 lbs fully ripe **tomatoes**

2 medium **onions**

2 cloves **garlic**

salt

1 lb **pappardelle**

3 tablespoons **olive oil**

2 tablespoons **balsamic vinegar**

freshly ground **black pepper**

sugar

½ cup **Parmesan cheese**, in one piece

2 tablespoons **ricotta cheese**

Preparation
SERVES 4

1 Clean and wash the arugula and dry in a salad spinner. Wash the tomatoes; blanch in boiling water, core and dice.

2 Peel and finely chop the onions. Peel and finely chop the garlic cloves.

3 Bring plenty of water to the boil, add salt, drop in the pappardelle and cook according to the instructions on the package until the pasta is al dente.

4 Meanwhile heat the oil in a frying pan, add the onions and garlic and cook until transparent. Add the diced tomatoes and cook with the other ingredients for about 8 minutes. Season with balsamic vinegar, salt, pepper and sugar, and keep the mixture warm.

5 Slice the Parmesan into thin pieces with a cheese slicer.

6 Strain the pappardelle into a sieve, allow to drain and dress with the tomato sauce. Mix in the arugula leaves and the ricotta, and scatter the Parmesan slices on top, and serve.

Sun-ripened tomatoes give this sauce its special taste. In winter it is best to use canned tomatoes, as their flavor is better than that of out-of-season tomatoes.

Saffron Pasta
with Green Vegetables

Preparation
SERVES 4

1 Combine the flour, egg yolks, eggs, ½ teaspoon salt, saffron and 1 tablespoon warm water, and knead to a smooth dough (see page 8). Shape the dough into a ball, wrap in plastic wrap and leave to rest for at least 30 minutes.

2 Meanwhile wash the vegetables. Clean the broccoli, divide into florets and peel the stalk. Quarter the zucchini lengthwise and cut into small pieces. Snip off the ends of the sugar snaps. Peel the lower third of the asparagus and cut diagonally into pieces.

3 Heat enough salted water in a saucepan to blanch one type of vegetable after the other. After blanching, rinse with ice-cold water and allow to drain thoroughly.

4 Roll the pasta dough out thinly and cut into wide ribbons. Cook in plenty of boiling water until al dente, and strain into a sieve. Melt the butter in a saucepan until it foams, and add the vegetables. Pour in the stock and add salt and pepper. Mix in the pasta, chives and Parmesan.

Ingredients

2 cups **all-purpose flour**

4 **egg yolks** · 2 **eggs**

salt · 1 pinch ground **saffron**

5 oz, about 2 cups, **broccoli**

1 small **zucchini** · ¼ lb **snow peas**

¼ lb **asparagus** · 4 tablespoons **butter**

6-8 tablespoons **vegetable stock**

½ tsp **saffron**

freshly ground **black pepper**

a few fresh **chives**

½ cup freshly grated **Parmesan cheese**

Ingredients

6 small **artichokes**

juice of ½ **lemon**

salt

1 lb **penne rigate**

3 tablespoons **olive oil**

1 peeled **garlic clove**

2 tablespoons **butter**

⅓ cup dry **white wine**

freshly ground **black pepper**

2 tablespoons finely chopped
fresh **parsley**

½ cup freshly grated **Parmesan cheese**

Penne
with Artichokes

Preparation
SERVES 4

1 Remove the outer leaves from the artichokes and cut off the stalk and the hard tips of the leaves with a sharp knife. Scrape out the chokes with a small spoon, and cut the artichokes into slices. Immediately place in a bowl with lemon water to avoid discoloration.

2 Bring plenty of water to the boil, add salt, drop in the penne and cook according to the instructions on the package until the pasta is al dente.

3 Meanwhile heat the oil in a frying pan and fry the garlic until it is golden brown. Remove the garlic, then add the artichokes and fry over a high heat until golden brown. Add the butter, pour in the white wine, cover and cook for a few minutes over a low heat.

4 Season with salt and pepper and add the well-drained penne along with the freshly chopped parsley. Mix thoroughly, scatter with Parmesan and serve.

Spaghetti
with Asparagus

Very little effort makes for a great result: Asparagus in a creamy sauce is a quick,
uncomplicated way to spoil yourself, as well as your guests

Ingredients

2 lbs **asparagus**

2 **shallots**

salt

1 lb **spaghetti**

2 tablespoons **butter**

¾ cup **vegetable stock**

1 cup **mascarpone cheese**

freshly ground **black pepper**

1 bunch **watercress**

Preparation
SERVES 4

1 Wash the asparagus, peel the lower third and cut into pieces
   about 1 ½ inches long. Peel and finely chop the shallots.

2 Bring plenty of water to the boil, add salt, drop in the spaghetti
   and cook according to the instruction on the package until the
   pasta is al dente.

3 Meanwhile melt the butter in a saucepan and cook the shallots in
   it until transparent. Add the asparagus and cook with the shallots
   for a short time. Pour in the vegetable stock and stir in the
   mascarpone. Simmer for about 10 minutes, then season with salt
   and pepper.

4 Strain the spaghetti into a sieve, allow to drain and mix with the
   sauce.

5 Wash the watercress thoroughly, cut off the leaves and stir into
   the mixture or, alternatively, tie into little bunches and use as a
   garnish.

**The mascarpone can be replaced by
cream cheese. The sauce will have extra
flavor if you use crème fraîche with
herbs, black pepper or horseradish.**

Spaghetti
with Sicilian Vegetables

A colorful pasta delight from southern Italy: In this recipe,

braised peppers with a fine vinegar accent are the key

Ingredients

½ lb each of **red, green** and **yellow peppers**

2 medium white **onions**

4 tablespoons **olive oil**

3 tablespoons **red wine vinegar**

1 lb can peeled **tomatoes**

1 tablespoon **balsamic vinegar**

sugar · **salt**

freshly ground **black pepper**

1 lb **spaghetti**

¼ cup **capers**

¼ lb **pecorino cheese**, in one piece

Preparation
SERVES 4

1 Halve the peppers lengthwise, seed and core. Wash the halves of pepper and cut into lozenge-shaped pieces about ¾-inch wide. Peel the onions and cut lengthwise into broad slices.

2 Heat the oil in a large saucepan and cook the onions and pieces of pepper in it for a few minutes. Add the red wine vinegar and tomatoes, and chop the tomatoes roughly with a fork. Season the vegetable mixture generously with balsamic vinegar, sugar, salt and pepper.

3 Bring plenty of water to the boil, add salt, drop in the spaghetti and cook according to the instructions on the package until the pasta is al dente.

4 Meanwhile simmer the vegetables over a low heat. After about 15 minutes, stir the capers into the vegetables. Allow the mixture to simmer for about 20 minutes, stirring occasionally.

5 Using a cheese slicer, slice the pecorino into fine shavings. Strain the spaghetti into a sieve and allow to drain. Arrange on a platter with the vegetables and garnish with the cheese and a few sprigs of fresh thyme if desired.

The vegetables will be even more aromatic if you stir in a few finely diced sun-dried tomatoes preserved in oil. For a hotter sauce, add a chopped red chili.

Pasta with Fish and Meat

Lasagne Sheets
with Vegetables and Shrimp

Here at last we have a layered pasta dish: An elegant one made with shrimp
and a white wine sauce for special occasions

Ingredients

4 large **carrots**

1 bunch **scallions**

3 tablespoons **butter**

1 lb **shrimp**, cleaned

salt

freshly ground **black pepper**

8 **lasagne sheets**

1 tablespoon **vegetable oil**

2 **shallots**

1 cup dry **white wine**

1 cup **crème fraîche** or
sour cream

juice of ½ **lemon**

Preparation
SERVES 4

1 Peel the carrots, clean and wash the scallions. Slice or dice the
carrots and cut the scallions diagonally into small pieces. Melt
2 tablespoons of the butter in a saucepan, add the vegetables and
cook until al dente.

2 Wash the shrimp thoroughly in cold water and dry with paper
towels. Add to the vegetables and cook with them for a short
time. Season generously with salt and pepper and leave to stand
in a warm place.

3 Cook the lasagne in plenty of boiling water with the oil until they
are soft (this applies even to lasagne that requires no pre-
cooking!). Take the sheets of pasta out of the water one by one
with a skimmer, laying them side by side on a teatowel to drain.

4 Meanwhile peel and finely chop the shallots. Cook in the
remaining butter, add the white wine and boil until reduced by
half. Stir in the crème fraîche and simmer for 2 more minutes.
Season with salt, pepper and lemon juice.

5 Cut the lasagne sheets in half, and using 4 half sheets per portion,
layer on pre-warmed plates with the shrimp, vegetables and
shallot sauce.

CERTIFICATE OF ATTENDANCE

THIS CERTIFIES THAT

Serrano Yenny

HAS COMPLETED AN ESL COURSE IN THE
ENGLISH LANGUAGE INSTITUTE
AT NASSAU COMMUNITY COLLEGE

COURSE NAME **Pronunciation For Beginning**

COURSE NUMBER CE5062 B1

04/28/2002
DATE

SPRING 2002
SEMESTER

PROFESSOR LEONARD DURSO
ESL PROGRAM COORDINATOR

Conchiglie
with Trout and Fennel

Simply irresistible: Combined with aniseed liqueur, fennel and trout fillet, ordinary pasta turns into a gourmet dish

Ingredients

2 leeks

1 bulb **fennel**

1 bunch fresh **tarragon**

salt

1 lb **conchiglie**

2 tablespoons **butter**

4 tablespoons **Pernod** or **Sambuca**

6 tablespoons **heavy cream**

4 smoked **trout fillets** (about 1 lb)

freshly ground **black pepper**

Preparation
SERVES 4

1 Clean and wash the leeks and fennel, then cut into thin slices. Set aside the fennel leaves for decoration.

2 Wash the tarragon and shake dry, then remove the leaves from the stems. Reserve a few leaves for decoration, and chop the remainder finely.

3 Bring plenty of water to the boil, add salt, drop in the conchiglie and cook according to the instructions on the package until the pasta is al dente.

4 Meanwhile melt the butter in a saucepan, add the sliced leeks and fennel and cook for about 4 minutes. Pour in the aniseed liqueur and the cream, and simmer the vegetable sauce for 5 minutes over a low heat.

5 Cut the trout fillets diagonally into slices about ½-inch wide. Add the pieces of fish and the chopped tarragon to the sauce, and simmer for a short time. Season with salt and pepper.

6 Strain the conchiglie into a sieve and allow to drain. Dress with the sauce, and serve garnished with the fennel and tarragon leaves.

A refined variation on the trout sauce: Instead of the fennel bulb, use 1 bunch each of arugula and flat-leaf parsley, and then flavor the sauce with lemon juice instead of the aniseed liqueur.

Spaghetti
with Shrimp and Tomatoes

Preparation
SERVES 4

1 Drain the artichoke hearts on paper towels and quarter lengthwise. Wash the tomatoes then blanch in boiling water, skin, core and cut into small dice.

2 Wash the shrimp thoroughly and dab dry. Clean and wash the scallions, then cut into fine rings.

3 Bring plenty of water to the boil, add salt, drop in the spaghetti and cook according to the instructions on the package until the pasta is al dente.

4 Meanwhile heat the oil in a wide frying pan, add the onions and cook until soft. Throw in the shrimp and artichokes and cook with the onions for a short time. Add the diced tomatoes and also cook briefly with the other ingredients.

5 Stir in the sherry, cream and green peppercorns. Season generously with salt and pepper.

6 Strain the spaghetti into a sieve and allow to drain. Dress with the sauce and garnish with the tarragon leaves.

Ingredients

8 marinated **artichoke hearts**

4 large **tomatoes**

½ lb **shrimp**, cleaned

3 **scallions**

salt · 1 lb **spaghetti**

2 tablespoons **olive oil**

6 tablespoons dry **sherry**

1 cup **heavy cream**

2 tablespoons **green peppercorns** in brine

pinch **cayenne pepper**

a few fresh **tarragon** leaves

Ingredients

2 lbs **clams**, in their shells

1 medium **tomato**

4 tablespoons **olive oil**

2 finely chopped **garlic cloves**

1 lb **vermicelli**

salt

½ bunch **flat-leaf parsley**

freshly ground **black pepper**

Vermicelli
with Clams

Preparation
SERVES 4

1 Wash and clean the clams. Discard the mussels that do not close when tapped.

2 Wash the tomatoes, blanch in boiling water, skin, core and dice. Heat 2 tablespoons of the oil and cook the garlic until transparent. Add the mussels, cover and cook for about 5 minutes, until the mussels open. Remove the mussels from their shells and strain the cooking liquid through a cheesecloth-lined sieve into a bowl.

3 Following the instructions on the package, cook the vermicelli in plenty of boiling water until it is al dente.

4 Meanwhile wash the parsley, shake dry and chop the leaves finely. Heat the remaining oil and cook the tomatoes in it. Add the mussels, cooking liquid and parsley, heat the whole mixture for about 3 minutes, then season with salt and pepper. Strain the vermicelli into a sieve, allow to drain and serve with the mussel sauce.

Strozzapreti
with Salmon and Cream Sauce

An excellent combination for guests: Pasta with smoked salmon and
a creamy herb sauce guarantee exquisite culinary delights

Ingredients

1 lb **strozzapreti** or **pennette**

salt

1 bunch fresh mixed **herbs**
(e.g. basil, oregano, rosemary)

1 tablespoon **butter**

1 cup **heavy cream**

2 tablespoons **lemon juice**

1 lb **smoked salmon**

freshly ground **black pepper**

Preparation
SERVES 4

1 Following the instructions on the package, cook the strozzapreti
in plenty of boiling water until it is al dente.

2 Meanwhile wash the herbs, shake dry and pull the leaves off the
stems. Set aside a few leaves for decoration, then cut the
remainder into fine strips.

3 Melt the butter in a frying pan. Add the herbs and cook for a short
time. Pour in the cream and lemon juice and cook the whole
mixture for about 4 minutes.

4 Cut the salmon into strips and briefly warm up in the sauce.
Season with salt and pepper.

5 Strain the strozzapreti in a sieve and allow to drain. Mix with the
sauce and serve garnished with the reserved herbs.

**A tip for very special occasions:
This dish is even finer if you use
watercress instead of the herbs
and decorate the dressed pasta with
edible nasturtium flowers.**

Herb Pasta
with Fish Sauce

A feast for the eye as well as the tastebuds:

Whole herbs inside homemade pasta add the final touch to this recipe

Ingredients

2 cups **all-purpose flour**

3 **egg yolks** · 1 **egg**

salt

a few **nasturtium flowers** and **leaves**

½ lb fresh **salmon fillet**

4 loose **scallops**

6 **shrimp**

¾ cup **clam juice**

1 cup **heavy cream**

freshly ground **black pepper**

½ teaspoon **saffron**

1 pinch **cayenne pepper**

3 tablespoons **olive oil**

2 tablespoons **Noilly Prat** vermouth

3 tablespoons **butter**

Preparation

SERVES 4

1 Combine the flour, egg yolks, egg, ½ teaspoon salt and 1 tablespoon warm water, knead to a pasta dough (see page 8), and roll out thinly using a pasta machine or a floured rolling pin.

2 Lay nasturtium flowers and leaves on half of each strip of pasta, fold over the other half, and once again run through the pasta machine at the same setting as before, or roll to the same thickness with the rolling-pin.

3 Cut the sheets of dough into broad strips about 1-inch wide. Dust the herb pasta with flour and leave to rest for at least 30 minutes.

4 For the fish sauce, cut the salmon into 1-inch pieces. Wash, peel, and de-vein the shrimp.

5 Cook the clam juice with the cream, pepper, saffron and cayenne pepper over a strong heat until the mixture has reduced to a thick consistency.

6 Heat 2 tablespoons of the oil in a frying pan and fry the shrimp in it for 2 minutes. Add the pieces of scallop and salmon and briefly toss with the shrimp. Pour in the vermouth, allow to reduce and mix in with the reduced fish sauce.

7 Cook the herb pasta in boiling salted water with the remaining tablespoon of oil until it is al dente. Strain into a sieve and allow to drain. Melt the butter in a saucepan until it foams, and toss the pasta in it for a short time. Pour the fish sauce over the pasta.

Pappardelle
with Turkey Ragout

A classic sauce that bewitches even connoisseurs: Turkey breast braised with red wine
and mushrooms brings a touch of la bella Italia to your table

Ingredients

3 dried **porcini mushrooms**

1 lb boneless, skinless
turkey breast

5 oz **turkey livers**

1 **onion**

2 cloves **garlic**

salt · 1 lb **pappardelle**

2 tablespoons **olive oil**

½ cup **red wine**

1 cup **vegetable stock**

1 tablespoon **tomato paste**

4 tablespoons **heavy cream**

2 sprigs fresh **rosemary**

1 teaspoon **red wine vinegar**

freshly ground **black pepper**

Preparation
SERVES 4

1 Place the dried mushrooms in a small bowl, pour boiling water over them and leave to soak for a few minutes. Strain the mushrooms into a sieve, reserving the water they have been soaked in.

2 Wash the turkey breast and livers, dab dry with paper towels and cut into slices. Peel and finely chop the onion and garlic cloves.

3 Bring plenty of water to the boil, add salt, drop in the pappardelle and cook according to the instructions on the package until the pasta is al dente.

4 Meanwhile heat the oil in a saucepan and fry the meat and livers. Add the onion, garlic and mushrooms, and cook all the ingredients for about 3 minutes.

5 Pour in the red wine, stock and about ½ cup of the reserved mushroom water. Add the tomato paste, cream and 1 sprig of rosemary, and simmer the whole mixture for a further 8 minutes. Season with red wine vinegar, salt and pepper.

6 Strain the pappardelle into a sieve and allow to drain. Toss with the turkey sauce, removing the sprig of rosemary before serving. Garnish with the remaining rosemary needles.

Spaghetti
with a Lemon and Lamb Sauce

An original pasta idea with style: Gently braised lamb is combined here
with crisp dandelion leaves

Ingredients

1 lb **lamb** from the leg

3 slices **bacon**

1 large **onion**

1 bunch yellow **dandelion leaves**
(see note)

2 tablespoons **olive oil**

1 clove **garlic**

salt · 1 lb **spaghetti**

½ cup **white wine**

1 cup **vegetable stock**

freshly ground **black pepper**

freshly grated **nutmeg**

1 teaspoon grated **lemon peel**

⅔ cup **crème fraîche** or
sour cream

6 tablespoons **lemon juice**

Preparation
SERVES 4

1 Dice the lamb and bacon into small pieces. Peel and finely chop the onions. Clean and wash the dandelion leaves, and shake dry.

2 Heat the oil in a frying pan, add the diced meat and bacon and fry for about 5 minutes. Pour off the juices and reserve them. Peel and finely chop the garlic, add to the pan along with the onions and cook all the ingredients together for a short time.

3 Bring plenty of water to the boil, add salt, drop in the spaghetti and cook according to the instructions on the package until the pasta is al dente.

4 Meanwhile add the reserved juices, wine and stock to the sauce, and season with salt, pepper, nutmeg and lemon peel. Allow the lamb ragout to simmer for a further 10 minutes.

5 Stir in the crème fraîche and lemon juice, and simmer over a low heat for 10 more minutes.

6 Strain the spaghetti into a sieve and allow to drain. Toss with the lamb sauce and the dandelion leaves.

If you cannot find yellow dandelion leaves, substitute arugula or watercress instead.

Rotelle
with Chicken Breasts

Preparation

1 Wash the parsley and shake dry. Reserve some for garnish. Remove the leaves from the remaining stems and chop finely.

2 Bring plenty of water to the boil, add salt, drop in the rotelle and cook according to the instructions on the package until the pasta is al dente.

3 Meanwhile fry the chicken breast fillets in 2 tablespoons of the oil until golden brown on both sides. Season with salt and pepper.

4 Remove the meat from the frying pan. Cook the onions and ginger in the remaining oil. Add the stock and lemon juice. Stir in the mascarpone and allow the sauce to reduce somewhat. Season with salt and pepper and stir in the chopped parsley.

5 Fry the parsley stems for a short time in the remaining oil. Strain the rotelle and allow to drain. Toss with the sauce, the cut-up chicken breasts and the parsley, and if desired, garnish with lemon zest.

72

Ingredients

1 finely chopped large **onion**

2 bunches fresh **flat-leaf parsley**

salt · 2 ¾ cups **rotelle**

2 boneless, skinless **chicken breasts**

6 tablespoons **olive oil**

freshly ground **black pepper**

1 teaspoon chopped fresh **ginger**

¾ cup **vegetable stock**

1 tablespoon **lemon juice**

2 tablespoons **mascarpone cheese**

Ingredients

1 ¼ lbs **veal cutlets**

1 **shallot** · ½ lb **carrots**

1 organically grown **lemon**

3 tablespoons **olive oil**

salt · 1 lb **spaghetti**

2 peeled **garlic cloves**, crushed

½ cup dry **white wine**

½ cup **vegetable stock**

4 tablespoons **crème fraîche** or
sour cream

½ teaspoon **saffron strands**

2 tablespoons **capers**

freshly ground **black pepper**

3 tablespoons **caper pods**

Spaghetti
with Veal

Preparation
SERVES 4

1 Cut the veal into strips. Peel and chop the shallot. Peel the carrots and cut into julienne. Wash and slice the lemon.

2 Heat the oil and fry the meat in it for about 4 minutes, stirring continuously. Remove from the pan and keep in a warm place.

3 Bring plenty of water to the boil, add salt and spaghetti and cook according to the instructions on the package until the pasta is al dente. Meanwhile cook the shallots and carrots in the fat left in the pan, add the garlic, then pour the wine and stock onto the mixture. Add the crème fraîche, saffron, capers with a little caper liquid, and 2 slices of lemon. Cover and allow to simmer for 6 minutes.

4 Finally add the veal and season with salt and pepper. Drain the spaghetti and serve with the sauce, caper pods and lemon slices.

Spaghetti
with Parma Ham

A special treat for lovers of Italian cuisine:

Spaghetti with the world-famous air-dried ham from Emilia-Romagna

Ingredients

1 lb **spaghetti**

salt

¼ lb cooked **ham**, in one piece

¼ lb **pearl onions**, about 5-6

1 bunch fresh **basil**

3 tablespoons **olive oil**

1 clove **garlic**

¼ lb **Parma ham**, in thin slices

¼ lb **Parmesan cheese**,
in one piece

freshly ground **black pepper**

Preparation
SERVES 4

1 Following the instructions on the package, cook the spaghetti in plenty of boiling water until it is al dente.

2 Meanwhile cut the cooked ham into small cubes. Peel the pearl onions. Wash the basil, shake dry and remove the leaves from the stems. Set aside 2 tablespoons of the leaves for decoration, then cut the remainder into strips.

3 Heat the oil in a large frying pan, and fry the cubes of ham and the onions in it for about 6 minutes. Peel and finely chop the garlic, and add to the mixture.

4 Using a vegetable parer or a cheese slicer, slice the Parmesan cheese into rough shavings. Strain the spaghetti into a sieve and allow to drain. Along with the Parma ham and up to 2 tablespoons of the Parmesan, add the pasta to the frying pan and mix with the other ingredients. Cook for a further 3 to 4 minutes, then season with salt and pepper.

5 Mix in the strips of basil. Scatter the ham and spaghetti mixture with the rest of the basil leaves and Parmesan, and serve.

Pappardelle
with Duck Breast

Quick to cook, juicy and tender: For this rich pasta sauce,

nothing but the best part of the duck will do

Ingredients

1 large **white onion**

2 cloves **garlic**

2 **duck breast fillets**

salt

1 lb **pappardelle**

6 tablespoons **olive oil**

1-lb can crushed **tomatoes**

¾ cup **chicken stock**

freshly ground **black pepper**

2 tablespoons **balsamic vinegar**

1 bunch fresh **sage**

¼ lb **Parma ham**, in thin slices

Preparation
SERVES 4

1 Peel and finely chop the onions and garlic cloves.

2 Pull the skin off the duck breast fillets and cut crosswise into strips. (If preferred, cut into small pieces and fry until crisp).

3 Bring plenty of water to the boil, add salt, drop in the pappardelle and cook according to the instructions on the package until the pasta is al dente.

4 Meanwhile heat 2 tablespoons of the oil in a saucepan and fry the duck strips. Add the onions and garlic and fry for about 3 more minutes.

5 Pour in the crushed tomatoes and chicken stock. Season the sauce with salt, pepper and balsamic vinegar and bring to the boil.

6 Meanwhile wash the sage, shake it dry and pull the leaves off the stems. Fry the leaves briefly in the remaining oil. Strain the pappardelle into a sieve and allow to drain. Toss with the sauce, ham slices, and sage leaves.

Those who like sage can add a few leaves to the water used for cooking the pasta. This gives the pappardelle itself a slight flavor of sage. The same procedure can be used with other herbs.

Pappardelle
with Hare Ragout

Preparation
SERVES 4

1 Chop the hare and bacon very finely. Peel and finely chop the onions and garlic. Wash the celery and cut into fine slices. Wash the tomato, blanch with boiling water, skin, core and dice.

2 Heat the butter and oil, add the bacon and fry until cooked right through. Throw in the hare and fry over a high heat. Reduce the heat and mix in the prepared vegetables, then season with salt, pepper and thyme.

3 Pour in the wine and beef stock, cover, and braise the ragout over a low heat for about 2 hours. Finally season again with salt and pepper.

4 Following the instructions on the package, cook the pappardelle in plenty of boiling water until it is al dente. Strain the pappardelle into a sieve, allow to drain and mix with the ragout. Serve garnished with fresh thyme if desired.

Ingredients

1 lb boneless **hare** or rabbit

2 slices **smoked bacon**

1 **onion** · 1 clove **garlic**

1 stalk **celery**

1 **beefsteak tomato**

1 tablespoon **butter**

2 tablespoons **olive oil**

salt · freshly ground **black pepper**

½ teaspoon dried **thyme**

6 tablespoons dry **white wine**

½ cup **vegetable stock**

1 lb **pappardelle**

Ingredients

2 dried **porcini mushrooms**

1 **carrot** · 1 **onion** · 1 clove **garlic**

3 slices **smoked bacon**

2 stalks **celery** · 3 tablespoons **butter**

½ lb **ground beef**

2 tablespoons **tomato paste**

salt · freshly ground **black pepper**

1 cup canned **chopped tomatoes**

½ cup **vegetable stock** · ½ cup **red wine**

1 teaspoon dried **thyme**

1 teaspoon dried **oregano**

⅔ cup **heavy cream** · 1 lb **macaroni**

⅜ cup freshly-grated **Parmesan cheese**

Macaroni
alla Bolognese

Preparation
SERVES 4

1 Pour boiling water over the mushrooms and leave to soak for a few minutes. Peel and finely dice the carrot, onion and garlic clove. Also dice the smoked bacon and celery into small pieces. Melt the butter, add all the diced ingredients and cook. Separate the ground beef into pieces and gradually cook, stirring continuously.

2 Stir in the tomato purée and the drained, finely diced mushrooms. Season with salt and pepper. Pour the chopped tomatoes, stock and wine onto the mixture. Add the thyme and oregano, bring to the boil once, cover and simmer over a low heat. After about 1 hour, stir in the cream, remove the lid and simmer for another 30 minutes.

3 Following the instructions on the package, cook the spaghetti in plenty of boiling water until it is al dente. Strain into a sieve, allow to drain and serve with the sauce and Parmesan.

Stuffed and Baked Pasta

Lasagne Boats
with Shrimp

It's hard to imagine a more elegant, refined pasta dish than this: Pasta pockets
stuffed with vegetables and topped with shrimp

Ingredients

8-10 **lasagne sheets**

salt

2 tablespoons **olive oil**

12 **jumbo shrimp**, cleaned

juice of 2 small **limes**

1 bunch fresh **dill**

1 bunch **scallions**

1 ½ lbs, about 6 small, **zucchini**

1 tablespoon **clarified butter**

freshly ground **black pepper**

butter for greasing the
baking-dish

¾ cup **heavy cream**

½ cup **cream cheese**

2 **eggs**

Preparation
SERVES 4

1 Bring plenty of water to the boil, add salt and 1 tablespoon of the
oil, drop in the lasagne sheets and cook for about 6 minutes until
soft (this applies even to no-boil lasagne!). Remove the pasta
sheets one by one, and place in a bowl of cold water to prevent
them from sticking together.

2 Meanwhile wash the shrimp thoroughly and dry with paper
towels. Squeeze the lime juice over the shrimp, cover and place
in the refrigerator. Wash, shake dry and finely chop the dill.
Clean and wash the scallions and cut into rings. Clean and wash
the zucchini, and grate roughly with a grater.

3 Heat the clarified butter in a frying pan, add the grated zucchini
and cook for about 1 minute. Remove the zucchini from the pan
and mix with the chopped dill and scallion rings.

4 Pour the lime juice that has drained off the shrimp onto the
vegetables. Season the shrimp and vegetables generously with salt
and pepper.

5 Preheat the oven to 350°F. Take the lasagne sheets out of the
water, dry on tea towels and fold together lengthwise to form
pockets. Place the pockets side by side and open-side up in a
greased ovenproof dish.

6 Stuff the pasta pockets with the vegetables and cover with the
shrimp. Stir the cream together with the cream cheese and eggs,
and add salt and pepper. Pour the cream and egg mixture over
the lasagne pockets and bake for about 20 minutes on the middle
shelf of the oven. After 10 minutes' cooking, brush the shrimp
with the remaining oil.

Spinach Lasagne
with Tomato Sauce

The classic dish without meat: A hot favorite, baked in the oven
until crisp and layer for layer a real delight

Ingredients

1 shallot

2 cloves **garlic**

3 tablespoons **olive oil**

3 tablespoons finely chopped
sun-dried tomatoes in oil

1-lb can **tomatoes**

¼ cup **white wine** · **salt**

freshly ground **black pepper**

½ lb baby **spinach**

1 lb **ricotta cheese**

freshly grated **nutmeg**

2 tablespoons **butter**

2 tablespoons all-purpose **flour**

1 ½ cups **milk**

½ cup freshly grated **Parmesan
cheese**

½ lb **lasagne sheets**

½ lb **mozzarella cheese**,
thinly sliced

Preparation
SERVES 4

1 Peel and finely chop the shallot and the garlic cloves. Heat
2 tablespoons of the oil in a large frying pan, add the garlic, shallots and
chopped dried tomatoes and cook the mixture.

2 Pour in the wine and the canned tomatoes with their juice, and
crush the tomatoes with a fork. Heat the sauce over a medium
heat for about 10 minutes until it has reduced to a thick
consistency. Season generously with salt and pepper.

3 Clean and wash the spinach and blanch briefly in boiling, salted
water. Strain into a sieve, squeeze out well and chop finely.

4 Place the spinach in a bowl and mix with the ricotta. Season
generously with nutmeg, salt and pepper.

5 Preheat the oven to 350° F. For the cheese sauce, melt the butter
in a small saucepan and brown the flour in it until golden yellow.
Gradually add the milk, stirring continuously. Stir in the Parmesan
and simmer the sauce over a low heat for about 10 minutes, until
thickened.

6 Grease an ovenproof dish with the remaining oil, and fill it in
layers. First line the bottom of the dish with lasagne sheets and
spread with tomato sauce. Cover with lasagne, then add a layer
of the spinach and ricotta mixture. In this order, layer all the
ingredients into the dish. Pour over the cheese sauce, and finally
lay the mozzarella on top. Bake the lasagne on the middle shelf
of the oven for about 60 minutes until golden brown.

Ravioli
with Potato and Mint Stuffing

Preparation
SERVES 4 – 6

1 Combine flour, eggs, salt and some water to form a pasta dough (see page 8) and leave to rest. For the stuffing, cook the potatoes in their skins in a small amount of water. Strain, allow to drain, skin and mash with a potato masher while still hot.

2 Wash the mint leaves, dab dry and chop. Peel and chop the garlic. Mix the mashed potatoes with the ricotta, mint and garlic, and season with salt and pepper.

3 Roll the dough out thinly on a floured work surface. Spoon teaspoonfuls of stuffing about 2 inches apart on one half of the sheet of dough. Fold the other half over and gently press in around the stuffing.

4 Cut the ravioli out with a fluted dough-cutter. Cook the ravioli in plenty of boiling, salted water for about 4 minutes. Strain into a sieve, allow to drain and serve with melted butter and grated Romano cheese.

Ingredients

3 cups **all-purpose flour**

4 **eggs** · **salt**

1 lb **potatoes**

about 50 fresh **mint** leaves

1 clove **garlic**

1 cup **ricotta cheese**

freshly ground **black pepper**

6 tablespoons **butter**

¼ cup freshly grated **Romano cheese**

Ingredients

3 cups **all-purpose flour**

6 **eggs** · **salt**

½ lb **Swiss chard**

2 peeled **garlic cloves**

1 cup freshly grated **pecorino cheese**

freshly ground **black pepper**

½ cup **walnuts**

3 tablespoons **pine nuts**

½ bunch **flat-leaf parsley**

2 tablespoons **ricotta cheese**

2 tablespoons **olive oil**

Pansoti
with Swiss Chard Stuffing

Preparation
SERVES 4–6

1 Using flour, 4 eggs, salt and some water, prepare a pasta dough, and leave it to rest.

2 Clean, wash and briefly blanch the Swiss chard, rinse with cold water and chop finely. Mix in 1 pressed garlic clove, 2 eggs and the pecorino. Season with salt and pepper.

3 Roast the walnuts and pine nuts in a frying pan without fat. Wash the parsley, shake it dry and pull off the leaves.

Place the nuts, pine nuts, parsley, the second garlic clove and some salt in a mortar, and pound with a pestle. Mix with the oil and crushed ricotta, and season with salt.

4 Roll the dough out thinly on a floured work surface, and cut into 3-inch triangles. Place some stuffing on each triangle and press down on the edges. Cook the pansoti in salted water for about 4 minutes. Stir 2 tablespoons of the cooking water into the sauce, and serve with the pansoti.

Conchiglioni
with Asparagus Stuffing

This turns a meal into a banquet: Big shell-shaped pasta shells
with an extravagant, exquisite chicken and asparagus stuffing

Ingredients

½ lb conchiglioni · salt

½ lb white asparagus

sugar

¼ lb boneless, skinless
chicken reast

2 shallots

1 bunch fresh flat-leaf parsley

¼ lb mozzarella cheese

1 egg yolk

2 tablespoons breadcrumbs

freshly ground black pepper

butter for greasing the dish

6 tablespoons dry white wine

2 tablespoons heavy cream

½ cup freshly grated Romano
cheese

2 teaspoons butter

Preparation
SERVES 2

1 Following the instructions on the package, cook the conchiglioni
in plenty of boiling water until it is al dente. Strain into a sieve,
rinse with cold water and leave to drain.

2 Wash the asparagus stalks, remove the woody ends and peel
thoroughly. Cook for about 15 minutes in plenty of boiling salted
water with a pinch of sugar. Allow the asparagus to drain and cut
diagonally into slices.

3 Cut the chicken into small cubes. Peel and finely chop the
shallots. Wash the parsley and shake it dry, remove the leaves
from the stems and chop finely. Cut the mozzarella into fine dice.

4 Preheat the oven to 400° F. Mix the asparagus slices with the
chicken, mozzarella, shallots, parsley, egg yolk and breadcrumbs,
and season generously with salt and pepper.

5 Use a tablespoon to stuff the conchiglioni with the mixture, and
place the pasta shells side by side in a greased ovenproof dish.
Mix the wine with the cream and pour into the dish. Scatter the
Romano over the stuffed pasta, and cover with small pieces of
butter. Bake the conchiglioni on the middle shelf of the oven for
about 35 minutes until lightly browned.

Pasta
en Papillote

A surprise on the plate: Spaghetti cooked in little parcels

with tasty tomato sauce tastes twice as good

Ingredients

1 clove **garlic**

4 tablespoons **olive oil**

½-lb can peeled **tomatoes**,
drained

salt

freshly ground **black pepper**

1 lb **spaghetti**

1 lb fresh **tomatoes**

1 bunch fresh **flat-leaf parsley**

⅓ cup **black olives**, pitted

8 slices **pancetta**

8 **anchovy fillets** (in oil)

½ cup thin slices **Parmesan cheese**

Preparation
SERVES 4

1 Peel and finely chop the garlic. Heat 2 tablespoons of the oil in a frying pan. Cook the garlic until transparent and remove from the pan. Add the canned tomatoes to the garlic oil and simmer for 10 minutes, then purée in a blender or food processor. Season generously with salt and pepper, and simmer for about 10 more minutes. Preheat the oven to 400° F.

2 Following the instructions on the package, cook the spaghetti in plenty of boiling water until it is al dente.

3 Meanwhile wash the tomatoes, blanch in boiling water, skin, core and dice. Wash the parsley and shake it dry. Remove the leaves from the stems and chop finely. Slice the olives.

4 Strain the spaghetti into a sieve and leave to drain. Mix with the tomato sauce, diced tomatoes, olives and 1 tablespoon of the parsley. Coat 8 pieces of parchment paper (about 10-inch x 10-inch) with the remaining oil.

5 Shape the tomato and pasta mixture into 8 nests and place each one in the middle of a piece of the parchment paper. Top each with 1 slice pancetta, 1 anchovy fillet and some parsley. Fold the paper together over the stuffing.

6 Place the pasta packages on a baking sheet and cook for about 15 minutes on the second-from-bottom shelf of the oven. To serve, open the paper packages and scatter the nests with Parmesan shavings.

Lasagne Roulades
with Ricotta and Ham

Preparation

SERVES 4

1 Bring plenty of water to the boil, add salt and one tablespoon of oil, drop in the lasagne sheets and cook until soft (this applies even to no-boil lasagne!). Remove the noodles one by one and place in a bowl of cold water.

2 Cut the ham into cubes. Clean and wash the arugula, dry in a salad spinner and chop very finely. Peel the onion and garlic and also chop finely. Heat 1 tablespoon of the oil, add the onion and garlic and cook until transparent. Preheat the oven to 350° F.

3 Combine the onion mixture with the arugula, ricotta, eggs and 1 cup of the Parmesan, then season with salt, pepper and nutmeg. Allow the lasagne sheets to drain and thinly cover with the mixture. Roll up from the short side, then cut each roll into 3 pieces of equal size.

4 Place the pasta roulades into a greased ovenproof dish, scatter with the remaining Parmesan and top with small pieces of butter. Bake on the middle shelf of the oven for about 15 minutes until golden.

92

Ingredients

8 sheets **lasagne** · **salt**

2 tablespoons **olive oil**

½-lb piece **ham**

1 bunch **arugula** · 1 **onion**

2 cloves **garlic**

2 cups **ricotta cheese**

2 **eggs**

1 ½ cups freshly grated **Parmesan cheese**

freshly ground **black pepper**

freshly grated **nutmeg**

butter for greasing the dish

2 teaspoons **butter**

Ingredients

about 6 small **leeks**

salt · freshly ground **black pepper**

freshly grated **nutmeg**

16 **cannelloni** (requiring no pre-cooking)

2 tablespoons **olive oil**

1 tablespoon **tomato purée**

1-lb can peeled **tomatoes** (canned)

1 tablespoon dried **oregano**

sugar · **butter** for greasing the dish

½ lb **Romano cheese**

¾ cup **crème fraîche** or sour cream

Cannelloni
with Leek Stuffing

Preparation
SERVES 4

1 Clean and wash the leeks, then cut them into 16 pieces (the pieces should be the same length as the cannelloni). Blanch in boiling, salted water. Drain and season with salt, pepper and nutmeg. Stuff the cannelloni with the leeks.

2 Heat the oil, add the tomato purée, canned tomatoes without juice and oregano, and cook the mixture. Allow to reduce for about 20 minutes, then season with salt, pepper and some sugar.

3 Preheat the oven to 400° F. Pour the tomato sauce into a greased ovenproof dish and place the cannelloni on top.

4 Stir the cheese together with the crème fraîche, season with salt and pepper and spread over the cannelloni. Bake the cannelloni on the middle shelf of the oven for about 35 minutes, switching on the oven grill for the last 3 minutes if necessary.

Cannelloni
with Vegetable Stuffing

It's the combination that does it: Crisp summer vegetables, fine herbs and
piquant goat's cheese give this stuffing the right style

Ingredients

1 lb **tomatoes**

1 **onion** · ½ **carrot**

½ stalk **celery**

6 tablespoons **olive oil**

2 teaspoons dried **thyme**

salt

freshly ground **black pepper**

1 **eggplant** · 2 small **zucchini**

1 clove **garlic** · 1 **red chili**

1 teaspoon dried **oregano**

1 ¼ cups **goat's cheese**

24 no-boil **cannelloni**

butter for greasing the dish

½ cup freshly grated
Romano cheese

2 teaspoons **butter**

Preparation

SERVES 6–8

1 For the tomato sauce, wash the tomatoes, blanch in boiling water, skin, core and cut into small pieces. Peel the onion and carrot and dice finely. Wash and dice the celery.

2 Heat 3 tablespoons of the oil in a saucepan and briefly braise all the vegetables in it, except for the tomatoes. Add the tomatoes and 1 teaspoon of the thyme. Season the sauce with salt and pepper, cover and simmer for about 20 minutes.

3 For the filling, wash the eggplant and zucchini and cut into small cubes. Peel and finely chop the garlic. Halve, core and wash the chili, then cut it into fine strips.

4 Heat the remaining oil, add the eggplant and zucchini cubes, garlic and chili, and cook the mixture. Season with salt, pepper, the oregano and the remaining thyme, and leave to cool somewhat. Chop the goat's cheese roughly and stir in. Preheat the oven to 425° F.

5 Fill each of the cannelloni with 2 to 3 tablespoons of the vegetable and cheese mixture, and layer into a greased ovenproof dish. Spread the tomato sauce over the top. Scatter the cannelloni with the Romano, top with small pieces of butter and bake on the middle shelf of the oven for about 30 minutes until golden brown.

Index

Cannelloni with Vegetable Stuffing	94
Canelloni with Leek Stuffing	93
Conchiglie with Trout and Fennel	60
Conchiglioni with Asparagus Stuffing	88
Farfalle with Sorrel Sauce	38
Farfalle Salad with Tomatoes and Olives	25
Fettucine with Peppers	36
Fusilli Salad with Radicchio	14
Garganelli Salad with Broccoli and Tuna	16
Herb Pasta with Fish Sauce	66
Lasagne with Vegetables and Shrimp	58
Lasagne Roulades with Ricotta and Ham	92
Lasagne Pockets with Shrimp	82
Linguine with Balsamic Lentils	45
Macaroni alla Bolognese	79
Macaroni with Spinach and Ricotta Sauce	34
Pansoti with Swiss Chard Stuffing	87
Pappardelle with Duck Breast	76
Pappardelle with Gorgonzola Sauce	32
Pappardelle with Hare Ragout	78
Pappardelle with Olive and Basil Sauce	35
Pappardelle with Turkey Ragout	68
Pappardelle with Tomato and Arugula Sauce	48
Pasta en Papillote	90
Penne with Artichokes	51
Penne with a Herb and Cheese Sauce	44
Penne with Tomatoes and Pesto	40
Penne Salad with Salsa Verde	18
Ravioli with Potato and Mint Stuffing	86
Rotelle with Chicken Breasts	72
Rotelle Salad with Salami and Arugula	24
Saffron Pasta with Green Vegetables	50
Spaghetti with Basil	46
Spaghetti with Shrimp and Tomatoes	62
Spaghetti with Asparagus	52
Spaghetti with Veal	73
Spaghetti with Parma Ham	74
Spaghetti with Mushrooms and Mint	30
Spaghetti with Romano Cheese	41
Spaghetti with Sicilian Vegetables	54
Spaghetti with a Lamb and Lemon Sauce	70
Spaghetti Salad with Avocados and Shrimp	26
Spaghetti Salad with a Herb and Cream Sauce	12
Spaghetti Salad with Spinach and Potatoes	17
Spaghetti Salad with Tuna Sauce	20
Spaghettini with Sun-dried Tomatoes	42
Spinach Lasagne with Tomato Sauce	84
Strozzapreti with Salmon and Cream Sauce	64
Tortiglioni Salad with Squid	22
Vermicelli with Clams	63

© Verlag Zabert Sandmann, Munich

Graphic design: Georg Feigl, Verena Fleischmann, Barbara Markwitz

Recipes: ZS-Team

Editing: Kathrin Ullerich

Production: Karin Mayer, Peter Karg-Cordes

Lithography: inteca Media Service GmbH, Rosenheim

Printing & Binding: Officine Grafiche De Agostini, Novara

English translation: Translate-A-Book, Oxford, UK

American editor: Frances Cleary

Typesetting: Wakewing Typesetting Services, High Wycombe, UK

This edition published by Barnes & Noble, Inc.,
by arrangement with Zabert Sandmann.
2002 Barnes & Noble Books
M 10 9 8 7 6 5 4 3 2 1
Printed in Italy
ISBN 0-7607-2884-4

Visit us also on our Internet website at www.zsverlag.de

Photographic Credits

Cover photos: StockFood/Elizabeth Watt (front); StockFood/Susie Eising (back)

Walter Cimbal: 83, 89, 91, 92, 93; StockFood/Uwe Bender: 28–9; StockFood/Caggiano Photography: 85; StockFood/Susie Eising: 2–3, 4–5, 7/2 and 4 top left, 7/bottom right, 8, 9, 13, 15, 19, 21, 23, 25, 27, 31, 33, 34, 35, 39, 41, 43, 44, 45, 47, 49, 50, 51, 53, 55, 56–57, 59, 61, 62, 63, 65, 66–67, 69, 71, 72, 73, 75, 77, 78, 79, 80–81, 86, 87, 95; StockFood/S. & P. Eising: 6/right, 7/top left and top right, 10–11, 24; StockFood/Walter Pfisterer: 6/left, 7/3 top left; StockFood/Elizabeth Watts: 16, 17, 40